My First Pet Library from the **American Humane Association**

My First Guinea Pig and Other Small Pets

Enslow Elementary
an imprint of
Enslow Publishers, Inc.
40 Industrial Road
Box 398
Berkeley Heights, NJ 07922
USA

http://www.enslow.com

American Humane®

Protecting
Children & Animals
Since 1877

Linda Bozzo

American Humane®

*Protecting
Children & Animals
Since 1877*

Founded in 1877, the American Humane Association is the oldest national organization dedicated to protecting both children and animals. Through a network of child and animal protection agencies and individuals, the American Humane Association develops policies, legislation, curricula, and training programs to protect children and animals from abuse, neglect, and exploitation. To learn how you can support the vision of a nation where no child or animal will ever be a victim of willful abuse or neglect, visit www.americanhumane.org, phone (303) 792-9900, or write to the American Humane Association at 63 Inverness Drive East, Englewood, Colorado, 80112-5117.

● ●

This book is dedicated to my husband and daughters, who never stop believing in me, and to pet lovers everywhere.

● ●

Library of Congress Cataloging-in-Publication Data

Bozzo, Linda.
   My first guinea pig and other small pets / Linda
     Bozzo.
     p. cm. — (My first pet library from the American
  Humane Association)
   Includes bibliographical references and index.
   ISBN-13: 978-0-7660-2752-7
   ISBN-10: 0-7660-2752-X
   1. Pets—Juvenile literature. 2. Guinea pigs as
     pets—Juvenile literature. I. Title. II. Series:
     Bozzo, Linda. My first pet library from the
     American Humane Association.
   SF416.2.B69 2007
   636.088'7—dc22
                      2006014970

Printed in the United States of America

10 9 8 7 6 5 4 3 2 1

To Our Readers:

We have done our best to make sure all Internet Addresses in this book were active and appropriate when we went to press. However, the author and the publisher have no control over and assume no liability for the material available on those Internet sites or on other Web sites they may link to. Any comments or suggestions can be sent by e-mail to comments@enslow.com or to the address on the back cover.

Every effort has been made to locate all copyright holders of material used in this book. If any errors or omissions have occurred, corrections will be made in future editions of this book.

Illustration Credits: Nicole diMella/Enslow Publishers, Inc., pp. 3, 20; Laura Dwight / PhotoEdit, p. 9; iStockphoto, pp. 8, 27; Michael Newman / PhotoEdit, p. 10; Shutterstock, pp. 1, 4, 5, 6, 7, 11, 13, 14, 15, 16, 17, 19, 20, 22, 23, 24, 25, 26, 28, 29.

Cover Illustration: Shutterstock.

Contents

Choosing a Small Pet

Small animals can make great pets. Some people enjoy guinea pigs. Others like hamsters or gerbils. Rabbits and ferrets are also very popular. Did you know that many people keep rats and mice as pets?

This book can help answer questions you may have about picking a small pet. It will also help you learn how to care for the animal.

Guinea pigs can make great pets.

4

Some people keep rats as pets.

Where Can I Get a Small Pet?

Check with your local animal shelter to see if they have the pet you want. You can also ask a **vet**, or animal doctor. Make sure you get your pets from people who take good care of their animals. A healthy animal moves and looks around.

Make sure your pet looks healthy before taking it home.

Here are some things to look for:

- The cage should be clean.

- The animal should be alert when it is awake.

- The eyes should look clear.

- The nose and ears should look clean.

- The fur should be clean.

White Siberian hamster

What Will My New Pet Need?

Rabbits, ferrets, guinea pigs, and rats need wire cages with solid bottoms and wire tops. Hamsters, gerbils, and mice can be kept in a glass tank with a screened top. Ask your vet what size cage is right for your pet. Set up the cage or tank in a quiet place before you bring your pet home. Your pet will need a water bottle and a food dish. Your hamster, gerbil, rat, or mouse will need an exercise wheel.

This mouse lives in a wire cage with a solid bottom.

8

A person at the pet store can also tell you what kind of food and **bedding** is best for the animal you pick.

Bedding will be needed for the bottom of your animal's cage or tank.

Special toys will help to keep your new small pet busy and happy.

Your new pet will need special food and bedding.

Guinea Pigs

Guinea pigs are playful and enjoy being with people. They like to live with other guinea pigs so you may want to get more than one. It is better if they were raised together. Be sure you get two males or two females, or they will have lots of babies.

Your guinea pigs will need a cage large enough to run around in. Place bedding in the bottom of the cage.

Your small pet will need fresh water every day.

Guinea pigs like to eat carrots.

Guinea pigs need chew sticks to keep their teeth from growing too long.

You can buy special food called guinea pig pellets from the pet store. Guinea pigs also like fresh fruits and vegetables such as carrots and apples a few times a week. It is very important that guinea pigs get enough vitamin C. The easiest way to make sure your guinea pigs get enough is to buy it at a pet store and add it to their water.

Guinea pigs need attention every day. They also need to be **groomed**. Use a brush to keep your pet's fur looking great.

Guinea pig

13

Hamsters

Hamsters are very clean pets.

Adult hamsters like to live alone, so only keep one.

These animals sleep during the day and run around at night.

Hamsters need a **nesting box** with a small entrance to make them feel safe. They also need chew sticks to keep their teeth from growing too long.

You should feed your hamster at night.

Hamsters eat special hamster food from the pet store. They also enjoy fruits and vegetables as treats. Hamsters are **nocturnal** so it is best to feed your hamster at night.

Only keep one hamster in the cage.

Gerbils

Gerbils are fun to watch.

They like to live with other gerbils so you may want to get more than one. Two brothers or two sisters raised together are best.

Cover the bottom of the cage with bedding.

Their cage should have room for lots of tunnels and shelves for them to run around in.

Cover the floor of the cage with bedding.

Give your gerbils paper towel tubes, branches, and cardboard boxes to play with.

This small animal will need to eat food made just for gerbils. They also enjoy **dates**, carrots, and **alfalfa** as treats. Feed your gerbils at night when they are most active.

Gerbils eat pellets made for them.

Rabbits

Rabbits are gentle animals.

Part of the bottom of your rabbit's cage should be covered with cardboard to protect its feet. Bedding is used to cover the bottom of the cage.

Rabbits need to hop around. Let your rabbit out of its cage once a day. Always make sure the room is safe because rabbits like to chew on things like electrical cords.

To keep your new pet healthy, feed it rabbit pellets. You can also feed it some hay and fresh vegetables. A **salt block** can also be given to your rabbit. Rabbits like to lick, and salt helps them stay healthy.

Hold your
rabbit gently.

Hay, straw, and wood sticks for your rabbit to chew on will keep its teeth from growing too long.

Some rabbits can be trained to use a litter box.

Ask your vet which bedding is right for your pet.

Hay is one of the foods rabbits like to eat.

Rabbits come in many colors and sizes. This is a miniature lop.

Ferrets

Ferrets need a cage large enough for a litter box and nesting box. Ferrets like nesting and sleeping on something soft such as a cloth, old T-shirt, or towel.

Let your ferret run around outside its cage. Always watch your ferret! These small animals can get into a lot of trouble when loose.

Dark sable ferret

Ferrets need to visit the vet once a year for a checkup and a shot to keep them healthy.

Ferrets can be trained to use a litter box.

Ferrets eat special food made just for them. They can also eat some types of cat food. Your ferret will need a bath once every few months.

Ferrets sleep on soft things like cloth.

Rats and Mice

Rats are very smart. Mice can be gentle.

These animals enjoy boxes and tunnels to crawl through. Like hamsters, both rats and mice need a nesting box.

Give them chew sticks to keep their teeth from growing too long.

Feed your mice or rats special food that includes nuts and seeds. They enjoy fresh fruits and crackers as treats.

Mice and rats sleep in a nesting box.

One way to tell if a mouse is healthy is by its clear, bright eyes.

How Can I Keep My Small Pet Healthy?

A vet can help keep your pet healthy. You may want a vet to check your new pet before you decide to bring it home.

A vet can trim your pet's nails if they get too long. If your pet stops eating, drinking, or shows other signs of being sick, call your vet right away.

Wash your pet's cage, food dish, and water bottle every week. After the cage is dry, put new bedding at the bottom of the cage.

Clean your pet's cage every week.

This vet gives
medicine to a
guinea pig.

Have Fun Caring For Your New Pet

Always handle your new pet gently and with care. Wash your hands before and after you handle your pet. Whatever small pet you pick, you can have fun caring for it. A small pet can live for years with lots of love and proper care.

Teddy bear hamster

Always be careful
when handling
your small pet.

Words to Know

alfalfa—A plantlike hay that gerbils like to eat as a treat.

bedding—A material that is placed in the bottom of an animal's cage like hay or straw.

dates—A fruit from a palm tree.

groomed—When an animal has cleaned itself. Also when a person has cleaned and brushed an animal.

nesting box—A private place for a small pet to sleep.

nocturnal—Active at night.

salt block—A large, usually round block of salt that rabbits like to lick.

vet—Vet is short for veterinarian, a doctor who takes care of animals.

Read About

BOOKS

Hamilton, Lynn. *Caring for Your Ferret*. New York: Weigl Publishers, 2004.

Holub, Joan. *Why Do Rabbits Hop? And Other Questions About Rabbits, Guinea Pigs, Hamsters, and Gerbils*. New York: Dial Books for Young Readers, 2003.

Loves, June. *Mice and Rats*. Philadelphia, Penn.: Chelsea Clubhouse, 2004.

Nelson, Robin. *Pet Guinea Pig*. Minneapolis, Minn.: Lerner Publications, 2003.

Starosta, Paul. *Face-to-Face with the Hamster*. Watertown, Mass.: Charlesbridge, 2004.

INTERNET ADDRESSES

American Humane Association
<http://www.americanhumane.org>
Learn more about animals at this site.

ASPCA: Animaland
<http://www.animaland.org>
Learn more about small pet care from the ASPCA.

Index